CHRIS HOY

with Joanna Nadin

Piccadilly
P R E S S

Part of the Bonnier Publishing Group

Flying Fergus and friends illustrations by Clare Elsom

This brilliant bike book belongs to:

_____

and comes with
SIR CHRIS HOY'S
CYCLING CERTIFICATE
OF AUTHENTICITY

THE BEGINNING OF MY TROPHY COLLECTION... I DIDN'T KNOW THEN I'D BE ADDING OLYMPIC GOLD MEDALS!

First published in Great Britain in 2016 by
Piccadilly Press
80–81 Wimpole Street, London, W1G 9RE
www.piccadillypress.co.uk

A CIP catalogue record for this book is available from the British Library.

ISBN: 978–1–471–40525–9

Safety first: The exercises, examples and stunts contained within this book may be too
strenuous and/or dangerous for some people due to their personal physical circumstances.
The reader should make sure that they consult with a suitably qualified physician before
engaging in any of the exercises, examples and stunts of the nature depicted. Adult supervision
is encouraged when using cooking equipment and performing bike maintenance tasks. The
author and publisher take no responsibility for any injury that may occur through following any
instructions or attempting to recreate anything that is described in this book.

Words by Joanna Nadin and Sir Chris Hoy
Cover and interiors design by Dynamo Limited
Illustrations by Clare Elsom and Dynamo Limited
Original photography of Sir Chris Hoy by Bryn Lennon, Getty Images

© Alamy: pp. 17, 35 © Evans Cycles: pp. 6, 73, 135 © Getty Images (Bryn Lennon): pp. 2, 4, 5, 14,
29, 32, 34, 36, 37, 41, 50, 52, 60, 62–67, 72, 80–81, 92, 98, 116, 129, 134 © iStock: pp. 21, 24, 25, 30, 42,
42, 50, 60, 61, 69, 82, 87, 88, 95, 100–101, 103, 105, 108, 110, 112 © iStock (Signature): pp. 48, 106
© Shutterstock: pp. 17, 17, 26, 33 (Mitch Gunn), 35 (Mitch Gunn), 38, 38, 39, 45, 48, 50, 50, 60,
67, 69, 74–75, 88, 93 (Mitch Gunn), 94 (Mitch Gunn), 118, 128
Family photographs: pp. iv, 3, 7, 117, 118, 126, 132, by kind permission of Sir Chris Hoy
Every effort has been made to trace copyright holders, but the publishers
would be pleased to rectify any omissions.

With thanks to Evans Cycles for the use of the HOY Bonaly 24 Inch Kids Bike

Printed and bound by Stige Arti Grafiche, Italy

Piccadilly Press is an imprint of Bonnier Zaffre,
a Bonnier Publishing Company
www.bonnierpublishing.co.uk

FSC
www.fsc.org
MIX
Paper from
responsible sources
FSC® C019014

Contents

ON MY WAY TO
WINNING THE
KEIRIN WORLD CUP
GOLD MEDAL
IN LONDON, 2012

Welcome to the **Wonderful World of Cycling!**

I learned to ride a bike when I was six years old, after watching the film E.T. I'd never seen a BMX bike before, but as soon as I saw it on screen I was desperate to ride on one. That started my obsession with bikes, which eventually led me to the velodrome and Olympic success.

It doesn't matter what you use your bike for: riding to and from school, playing with friends, exploring the countryside, doing tricks or even racing, there's so much fun to be had.

You don't need to spend a huge amount of money to enjoy cycling, but if you choose the right bike, find your way around it and look after it, you'll get the most out of your time on two wheels.

The best thing about cycling is that you never outgrow it, so you can do it for as long as you want.

I'll be with you on your journey, alongside some of my Flying Fergus pals, with advice and top tips, so you can get the most out of your time on your bike.

Sir Chris Hoy

What This Manual Does

This book is designed to give you all the basic knowledge you need to get cycling safely, in parks, on cycle tracks and out on the road.

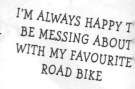

I'M ALWAYS HAPPY T
BE MESSING ABOUT
WITH MY FAVOURITE
ROAD BIKE

We'll help you choose a bike, if you don't already have one, walking you through all the different styles out there and what they're designed for, so you can work out which one suits you.

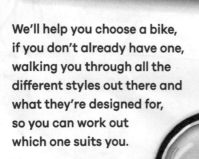

We'll let you know what kit you need, and what you don't, from helmets to hi-viz, and from bells to bottom-hugging shorts!

LOOK OUT FOR THE THESE FUN FACT BOXES FROM FERGUS AND THE GANG

Fergus's FASCINATING FACTS

The first bicycle, built in 1817, was called a Draisine, after its German inventor Karl von Drais. It was made of wood and had no pedals – a bit like a modern balance bike.

There are step-by-step guides on how to keep your bike in tip-top condition. And, as we all know accidents happen, we'll tell you how to fix it when things go wrong, so you're never stuck in the mud when the chain slips off or your front wheel gets a puncture.

WHENEVER YOU SEE THIS SYMBOL, FOLLOW THE LINK AND GO ONLINE TO FIND A VIDEO OF SIR CHRIS DEMONSTRATING TO HELP YOU ON YOUR WAY TO SUCCESS

GIVE WAY

Safety is a must, so there's loads of detail about how to keep safe when you're out and about, from what you wear to recognising road signs and sticking to the Highway Code.

WITH THE KIDS TRYING OUT THE HOY BIKES I'VE DESIGNED WITH EVANS CYCLES ESPECIALLY FOR YOUNGER RIDERS

And your bike's not the only thing you need to look after – if you're going to be a cyclist you need to make sure you're in good condition too. So we'll show you a few simple exercises to build strength and stamina, and how you can eat better to cycle better.

But first and foremost, cycling is about fun, right? So there's a whole chapter of brilliant ways to get the most out of your bike, from blinging it up, to trying out new tricks on it, to setting up a cycle club with your mates so you can all enjoy the ride.

TAKING SOME AIR IN MY BMX DAYS – LEARNING HOW TO BUNNY HOP IS A GREAT START!

Last of all we hand the manual over to you with our super cycle logbook. Here's where you can keep a record of all your rides, of routes you want to try, and of the tricks you've mastered. There's even stuff to do on a rainy day when you're stuck inside, with a plan to help you write your own cycling story, just like Fergus's.

SO TURN THE PAGE, GET STUCK IN, AND THEN, GET ON YOUR BIKE!

Fergus

First past the post is wee Fergus Hamilton – he may only be nine years old but he's already one of the top young cyclists in Scotland. And he didn't get where he is on a flash bike either, it's all down to practice, and his trusty set of second-hand wheels, which he did up all by himself. Okay, well maybe he had a bit of help from Grandpa Herc! Fergus's dream is to follow in the tracks of his hero and champion cyclist Steve "Spokes" Sullivan. But for now he'll settle on beating his arch-rival Wesley Wallace in the Districts.

Daisy

There isn't a bicycle fact that Fergus's best friend and team-mate Daisy doesn't know, so she'll be testing you on what you've learned along the way. It's amazing how much she's managed to cram in her head, given she only started cycling seriously a few months ago. Not that she didn't want to – more like she didn't have the chance, what with no bike, and a mum who was worried about crashes. But with the help of Fergus and Grandpa Herc, Daisy's got her own set of wheels now, and she always wears her helmet, so even Mum's happy. Well, as happy as Daisy's mum ever gets.

FIND OUT MORE ABOUT THE CHARACTERS AND THEIR ADVENTURES IN THE FLYING FERGUS BOOKS AT: WWW.FLYINGFERGUS.COM

Grandpa Herc

Grandpa Herc is a whizz at bike maintenance, so he'll be helping Chris show you how to keep your bike in tip-top condition. Once upon a time he was a canny racer himself, but now he stays behind the scenes as team coach and mechanic. And as if that wasn't enough, he runs a second-hand bike shop too, so he knows exactly how to help you if you want to get into doing up your own bike.

Minnie McLeod

Our Minnie may be small but she's a giant when it comes to fun on two wheels. An expert at balancing and bunny hops, she'll be walking (or riding) you through some easy tricks you can learn. And making sure you're safe when you try them out too.

FIND OUT MORE ABOUT THE CHARACTERS AND THEIR ADVENTURES IN THE FLYING FERGUS BOOKS AT: WWW.FLYINGFERGUS.COM

Calamity Coogan

Also on team Hercules' Hopefuls is Callum Coogan, better known as Calamity – by name and by nature! Prone to bumps and bashes, he needs all the safety help he can get, so he'll be learning with you as you find out about basic checks you can carry out before you set off, as well as the rules of the road.

Chimp

Last but not least comes Chimp. He may look like a mongrel, but he's as fit as a fiddle, and no dog can beat him when it comes to cheering our team on. He'll be showing you how you can exercise and eat well, two things all cyclists need to know. (Even if it does mean cutting down on a few sausages every once in a while, eh, Chimp?)

FIND OUT MORE ABOUT THE CHARACTERS AND THEIR ADVENTURES IN THE FLYING FERGUS BOOKS AT: WWW.FLYINGFERGUS.COM

Chapter 1

Choosing and Getting to Know Your Bike

Getting a new bike is an exciting moment no matter what age you are, but getting your very first bike is a real thrill you'll never forget.

My first bike was bought second-hand in a jumble sale for £5. Dad resprayed it and pimped it up to look and ride like a BMX. I absolutely loved it and it started a lifelong obsession. If you're buying a bike rather than getting a hand-me-down from a big brother or sister, you've got some choices to make about what kind of bike you want. This chapter will hopefully help you with that decision.

Whatever you get, make sure it's the right size, you wear a helmet when riding on it, and most importantly, you have fun!

Which Bike Tribe Are You?

There are hundreds of different bikes out there, and the choice can be overwhelming. Narrow it down by deciding which KIND of bike you want.

There are only a few different shapes of frame and wheels, designed especially for where and how they're ridden. So **mountain bikes** are tough with chunky wheels to make it easier to handle slippery surfaces and bumps when you're off the beaten track. **Road bikes** have a sleek, skinny shape and handlebars that force you forward in the saddle. Great if you're a speed freak. But there's more to choose from too. Have a look at the most popular and see which one suits you best – but bear in mind some of these are **specialist**, and can be expensive. If you're not sure what kind of cyclist you're going to be yet, choose a good all-rounder, like a **hybrid**. And remember, you're growing fast, which means other kids are too, so there are always some great second-hand bargains to be had, meaning you can get a lot higher spec for your money.

TURN THE PAGE TO FIND OUT MORE ABOUT THE DIFFERENT BIKES YOU CAN CHOOSE FROM.

ALL-ACTION MOUNTAIN BIKE

FAST AND LIGHT ROAD BIKE

MY SPECIALIST TRACK BIKE IN THE FINAL LAP OF THE ATHENS OLYMPICS IN 2004. MY FIRST GOLD MEDAL!

Mountain Bikes

Mountain bikes are built for tough, off-road tracks and wet weather. Flat, wide handlebars help keep riders stable and the big wheels have fat tyres with a deep tread, good for gripping muddy ground. They have lots of gears to help riders get up steep hills, and the front wheel forks often have suspension to absorb impact over bumps and jumps – a bit like springs. They can be great fun to ride, but bear in mind they're heavier than road bikes, and often don't have mudguards, meaning your clothes can get very messy!

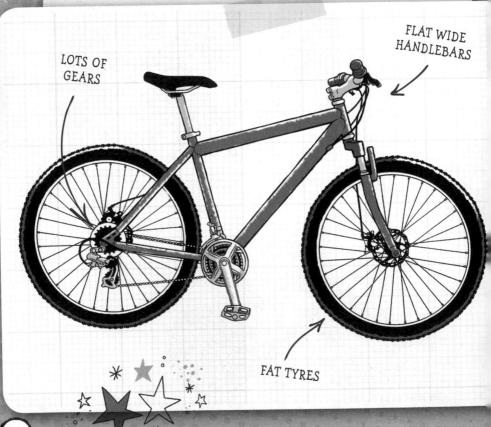

LOTS OF GEARS

FLAT WIDE HANDLEBARS

FAT TYRES

Road Bikes

Road bikes are designed for speed out on the streets. They have lightweight, streamlined frames, high-up saddles, and distinctive handlebars that drop down and under, meaning you can lean forward when you ride, which makes you go faster. The wheels are narrow with smooth tyres, so they go quickly over the road surface. Some pedals have toeclips, which lock your shoes in place. This may feel funny, but it means you can pull up on the pedal as well as push down, which gives you more power.

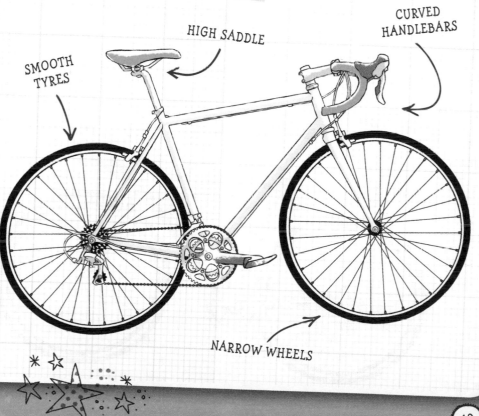

SMOOTH TYRES

HIGH SADDLE

CURVED HANDLEBARS

NARROW WHEELS

Cross Bikes or Hybrids

Hybrid means a cross between two things, and that's what hybrid bikes are. The most common kind is a cross between a road bike and a mountain bike, which is called a cyclo-cross. A cyclo-cross bike is designed to be ridden off-road on rough or muddy surfaces, just like a mountain bike, but is lighter, has no comfy suspension and has a riding position and handlebar set-up similar to a road bike. They are designed to be raced on cyclo-cross circuits so need to be light, nimble and strong. Because they don't usually have suspension, going over jumps isn't as smooth as on a mountain bike, but some hybrids often have mudguards, which should keep you cleaner and drier in the saddle. Hybrids can be a great bike to choose if you'd like to experience the benefits of a light and fast road bike, but with the durability of a mountain bike.

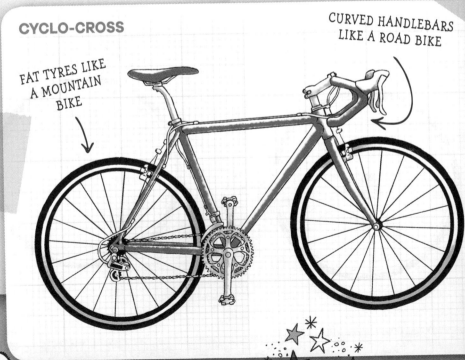

CYCLO-CROSS

CURVED HANDLEBARS LIKE A ROAD BIKE

FAT TYRES LIKE A MOUNTAIN BIKE

LIGHT ENOUGH TO CARRY

TOUGH ENOUGH FOR OFF-ROAD

URBAN HYBRID

REAR PANNIER RACK

LIGHTWEIGHT FRAME

BMX

BMX stands for Bicycle Motocross, after the motorbike sport that inspired it. BMX riders race over obstacles called humps, jumps and berms (which are banked curves) or compete to perform the best tricks. BMX bikes need to be smaller than other bikes so that riders have more control in the air. They also have sturdier frames and much smaller, fatter wheels than usual to absorb the impact when the bike hits the ground. But small wheels mean they're not great over long distance, and the size of the frame makes them uncomfortable after a while too. They often only have a rear brake, rather than both front and rear, so they're not necessarily suitable for use on the open road.

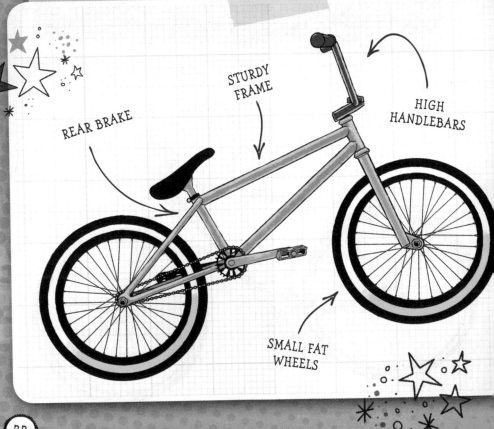

REAR BRAKE

STURDY
FRAME

HIGH
HANDLEBARS

SMALL FAT
WHEELS

Track Bikes

Track bikes or 'velodrome' bikes are built for one thing: speed. Everything about them is designed to cut resistance – that's the force from the air and ground that can slow you down. They only have one gear (because they never have to go uphill), no brakes, and often have aerodynamic wheels made from carbon fibre, which cut through the air quickly. They are the lightest of all types of bike. The saddle is positioned high up to force the cyclist to lean low over the handlebars, and the handlebars themselves often have extensions, meaning the rider's arms are as flat as possible.

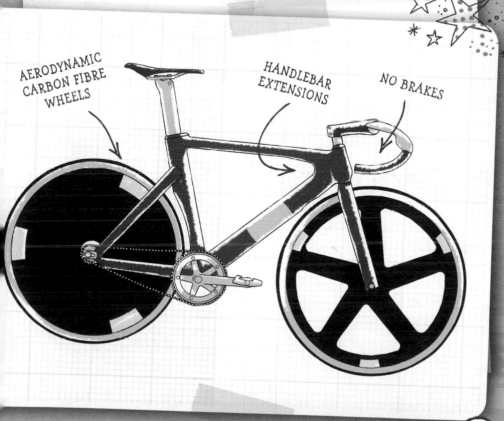

AERODYNAMIC CARBON FIBRE WHEELS

HANDLEBAR EXTENSIONS

NO BRAKES

Folding Bikes

Folding bikes are really great if you regularly make a journey that's too far to ride all the way - you can take your folded bike on a bus or train, then enjoy being in the saddle when you get off again. Folding bike frames look more like BMX bikes: they're small and chunky, and have much smaller wheels than road or mountain bikes. That's so they fold up into a compact shape to carry around. But the saddle and handlebars are at normal height, so the ride is as comfortable as it can be.

FRAME FOLDS IN HALF SO THE WHEELS ARE TOGETHER

Recumbent Bikes

Recumbent bikes are low and long, and have a very different cycling position, meaning you're almost lying back when you pedal. Because of their shape, they're much more aerodynamic, meaning you can go much faster for the same effort.

Daisy's DID YOU KNOW?

The world speed record for a bicycle is held by a recumbent bike.

Tandems

Tandems can be great fun, and having two people on board means you only have to do half the work. But if your cycling partner isn't about, then it means staying home, because riding a tandem alone can be dangerous!

Choosing the Best Bike

Once you've decided which kind of bike suits you, your next job is to make sure it's the right size. If it's too big or too small, you won't be able to ride it as fast or as well as you want, plus it's much easier to fall off a bike that's the wrong size.

Getting the size right

Children's bikes are usually measured by age and wheel size. But some people are tall for their age and some short, so the only way you'll really know if it fits is to sit on it. Even if you decide to buy a bike online, you can test out some sizes in a store so you'll know you're getting the right one.

**TURN THE PAGE TO FIND OUT
THE TOP THREE THINGS TO TEST**

Grandpa Herc's
WISE ADVICE

Sometimes people buying a bike for a growing child are tempted to choose a bike that's too big, for them to 'grow into'. Classic mistake! It can put your kid off cycling altogether, as the bike will be uncomfortable and difficult to ride. With some canny seat post and handlebar stem adjustments, the bike can be adapted to fit as your wee one grows. Also, by buying a good quality bike, it will last longer to either be passed on to a younger brother or sister, or sold second-hand to someone else.

1
Your leg should be almost straight when the pedal reaches its lowest point – that way you get the most power.

2
You need to be able to get the tips of your toes on the ground easily, to steady yourself before you set off and when you come to a stop.

The handlebars should be at a comfy height. Too high or too low and you won't be able to control the bike properly.

If the bike doesn't feel right at first, then try adjusting the saddle and handlebars up and down to get a better fit. If it still doesn't feel comfy and safe, or if your saddle and handlebars are already at the highest or lowest they can go, then it might be time to try another bike.

Chris's TOP TIPS

⚙ Go for a lightweight bike; it'll be easier to control and more fun to ride.

⚙ Avoid suspension unless you REALLY need it. Springy arms and legs and fat tyres can deal with most bumps that come your way.

⚙ Don't buy a bike that's too big, to 'grow into'. Get one that's the right size but that you can adjust the saddle and handlebars as you need to.

⚙ Unless you're really keen on one particular type of cycling, go for an all-rounder that can deal with all varieties of surfaces to ride on.

⚙ Make sure you get someone who knows how to set up a bike properly to check your bike is safe before riding on it.

DAISY'S QUICKFIRE QUIZ

Time to test your biking knowledge.
Answers are at the back of the book,
but no peeking! If you're stuck, check back
over the chapter – all the clues are there.

1. **Which has bigger wheels:
a mountain bike or a BMX?**

2. **Why do the pedals on some road
bikes have toe clips?**

3. **Which bike is best for going uphill:
a hybrid or a track bike?**

4. **Should your feet be flat on the floor,
toes touching the ground, or above the
ground with the saddle at the right height?**

5. **What type of bike holds the
world speed record?**

ANSWERS ON PAGE 158.

Chapter 2

Clothing, Kit and Caboodle

Having the right equipment can be crucial. It will make you a safer cyclist but it can be fun to wear and use too. Getting the most from cycling doesn't need to be expensive – not everything is essential.

To enjoy riding your bike you don't need to dress like I did when I used to race on the track. A good idea is to follow three basic rules - protect your head, be seen, and be comfortable.

IN MY TRACK KIT AT THE WORLD CHAMPIONSHIPS - HELMET, GLOVES AND PROTECTIVE VISOR

Helmet

ESSENTIAL

This is the most important piece of kit you'll buy. We need a hard layer to protect our skull, which in turn protects our brain inside – one of our most valuable organs! That's why it's worth spending a bit more to get something decent. And don't even think of getting a second-hand helmet unless you know exactly how it's been used. Any knocks weaken the structure, meaning your noggin won't get the protection it needs and deserves. Most helmets are made from the same material – polystyrene, which is light and shock-absorbing, covered in a bright, plastic shell. You'll notice a few holes too – these are called 'vents' and let air in to keep your head cool.

HARD PLASTIC SHELL

AIR VENTS TO KEEP COOL

SHOCK-ABSORBING POLYSTYRENE INNER

CE

MAKE SURE A NEW HELMET HAS A CE STICKER ON IT – THAT MEANS IT MEETS THE EUROPEAN SAFETY STANDARD.

SKATE
HELMET

MY AERODYNAMIC
GO-FASTER RACE HELMET

Helmets don't all look the same though –there are a few different styles to choose from. Mountain bike helmets sometimes have peaks, while other helmets designed for road riding will be much more sleek because it's hard to see through the peak when you're leaning forward. Some cyclists wear skate helmets – these are much rounder in shape than traditional helmets - great for stunt riders as they protect more of the back of the head. The most extreme shaped helmets of all are used by those racing against the clock on track or road. The distinctive 'pointed tail' and visor makes this type of helmet very aerodynamic for maximum speed. Don't worry too much about style at this stage though; a decent helmet will do the job whatever it looks like. The best rule to follow is to choose the right type of helmet for the kind of riding you will be doing.

A hand-me-down from someone you know is okay, but don't pick one up in a charity shop because you won't know how many times it's been crashed and bashed.

✿ Find the Right Fit

Once you've chosen your helmet, make sure it fits really well. The helmet should be snug so that, even without the straps done up, if you waggle your head it won't fall off. A good way to find the right helmet quickly is to measure the circumference of your head (that means all the way round). Get a tape measure and wind it round your head just above your ears. Make a note of the measurement so you can tell the bike shop. If the helmet is a tiny bit too big or small, adjust the retention system around the base of the helmet. This helps keep the helmet on your head if you crash.

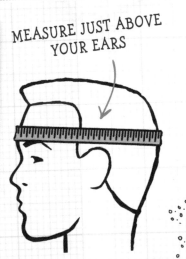

MEASURE JUST ABOVE YOUR EARS

Chris's TOP TIPS

Helmets can seem like a pain but they could save your life and you can get really cool ones so NO EXCUSES! I used to bling mine up with stickers called 'decals' so even if yours is plain you can make it stand out.

✿ Wear it Well

Once you've found a helmet that's snug, you need to tighten the chin strap. It should be tight enough to keep the helmet firmly in place, but not so tight it chokes you!

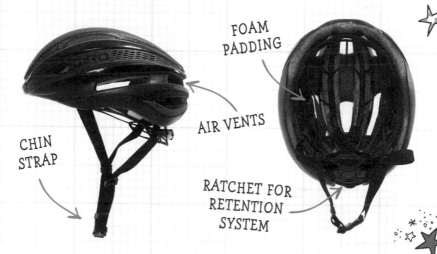

FOAM PADDING

AIR VENTS

CHIN STRAP

RATCHET FOR RETENTION SYSTEM

DO KEEP YOUR HELMET STRAIGHT

DON'T TILT YOUR HELMET ON YOUR HEAD

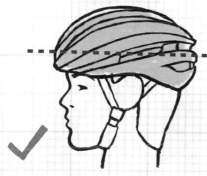

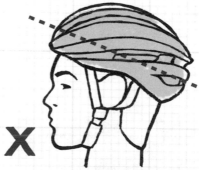

To keep your helmet in good condition clean it with soapy water and a cloth. If you do crash, check the helmet for cracks. If you find one, then the bin is the only way to go. Adult helmets should last five to ten years, but you'll probably grow out of yours way before that so if it starts to feel too tight, it's probably time to move up a size.

Bright Outerwear

Being seen on your bike is vital. You need other road users to notice you, so they can overtake you safely, or let you pass. It's a good idea to make sure you always wear bright clothing so you stand out, but it's especially important in bad weather or when it gets dark. You can buy special high-visibility neon jackets or sashes if you're going to ride when it's getting dark.

BRIGHT CLOTHES OR HIGH-VISIBILITY JACKETS HELP YOU STAY SAFE

Lights

Lights are another essential if you're riding at night or in bad weather. Not only will they help you see your way, they'll mean others can see you too. There are two kinds: battery-operated, and dynamo. Dynamo lights are connected to the wheel and use the power you create by pedaling to turn a tiny motor, which in turn switches the lights on. This means you'll never need to worry about changing batteries.

DYNAMO

Bell ESSENTIAL

You're not always going to get the cycle path or road to yourself, so a bell is a must. Bells are cheap, and you can find them in all bike shops. They attach to the handlebars – on the left-hand side if you're right-handed – with easy to fix nuts and bolts, but if you're buying your bike new you'll probably find one on there already.

Cycling Clothes

There's loads of exciting specialist clothing out there. It's designed for speed and comfort, so clothes are tight to make your shape more streamlined, but still keep you cool by 'wicking' sweat away from the body. They're usually designed with visibility in mind too, in bright colours or with patches or flashes of fluorescent fabric on them.

✿ Shorts

Special cycling shorts stop you getting saddle sore. The material is shiny, so it doesn't rub against your skin, and lots of them have padding in the bottom too, because sitting down for long periods can get painful!

✿ Jerseys

Like shorts, jerseys are tight. They can be long or short-sleeved and often come in team and country colours, so you can be a superfan when you're in the saddle.

✿ Shoes

If you're getting into mountain or road biking in a big way then eventually you'll want to get specialist shoes. Mountain bike shoes are rugged and can be worn for walking in as well. Road bike shoes are specially designed to be used with lock-in pedals and are very uncomfortable to walk around in. Until then, you're fine with normal boots or shoes as long as they have hard enough soles that you can push down properly. Don't choose anything too slippery, and wellies are a real no-no!

FITTED JERSEY

TO KEEP ME COOL
AND HELP ME
GO FASTER

ROAD BIKE
SHOES

TO LOCK MY
FEET INTO
THE PEDALS

TIGHT SHORTS
WITH PADDING

TO KEEP ME
COMFORTABLE IN
THE SADDLE

Pads

Pads aren't essential for day-to-day riding but if you're going to start trying out some tricks on your BMX or mountain bike then you'll need all the protection you can get. Knee and elbow pads come in pairs in different styles and sizes, so make sure you try before you buy. If you're really getting into off-roading, then you could always invest in body armour – these are vests that protect your chest and back, just like a helmet does.

GETTING THE RIGHT FIT IS THE MOST IMPORTANT THING TO REMEMBER – YOU NEED TO BE ABLE TO MOVE PROPERLY.

KNEE PAL

Chris's TOP TIPS

Don't think you have to have the latest kit to be a good cyclist – just get the basics right. All you really need to do is wear clothes that are bright and light, and preferably tight. Keep these tips in mind:

⚙ Trousers shouldn't flap about at the bottom; if they do, then you'll need to invest in some cycle clips to keep them in, or just tuck them into your socks, particularly on your right leg, which is always next to the chain.

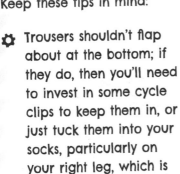

⚙ If the weather's chilly, then a few layers are better than one thick jumper. This makes it easier to move, and easier to take off a layer if the weather changes or you get hot from all the hard work.

⚙ It's worth getting a pair of gloves too. They'll keep your hands warm, help you grip the handlebars and brake levers tightly (sweaty hands can slip), and protect your palms if you have a tumble!

⚙ Lastly, make sure you're dressed for the weather. If it's rainy, wear a light mac. If it's hot, make sure you slap on some sun cream – as important as a helmet in protecting you from harm.

Bike Lock

The last thing you want is for someone to take a shine to your shiny new bike and nip off with it, so a bike lock is an essential piece of kit. There are two kinds: key locks and combination locks. Key locks use (you guessed it!) a key and combination locks mean you need to use a 3 or 4 digit number to operate the lock.

Daisy's DOS AND DON'TS

✿ DO keep the key safe if you're using a key lock, and DO keep a spare at home just in case you lose it.

✿ DO make sure the number for a combination lock is memorable — your birthday is a good bet, or the date you got your first bike.

- **DON'T** lock the bike to the saddle or wheels – they can be taken off easily. Make sure you **DO** lock to the frame of the bike.

- **DON'T** accidentally lock your bike to someone else's. They could get angry if they try to cycle off and find your bike attached to theirs!

Pump and ESSENTIAL Puncture Repair Kit

No one likes to think about accidents but they do happen, so carrying your pump and a puncture repair kit is essential unless you want a long walk home. These are cheap and can be bought from all bike shops, and they're light too, so if your pump isn't fixed to the frame, it's easy to pop in a rucksack. The puncture repair kit will even fit in your pocket. We'll tell you how to use it on pages 66-67.

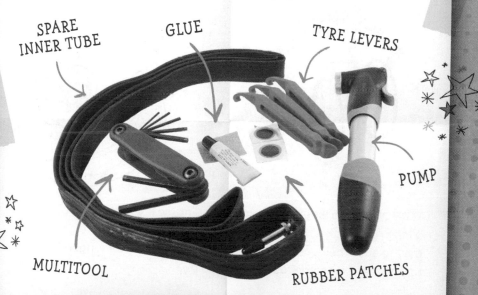

SPARE INNER TUBE

GLUE

TYRE LEVERS

PUMP

MULTITOOL

RUBBER PATCHES

Water Bottle and Snacks

Cycling makes you sweat, which means you lose water, so keeping hydrated is essential. Water bottles can be fixed to your bike or kept in your rucksack. But make sure they do contain water. Fizzy drinks are hard to swallow and not great for your health either – something cyclists have to think about. They might also pop the lid off the bottle as you ride along.

You'll also use a lot of energy when cycling, so if you're going out on a long ride, pack a few snacks for the journey. Bananas are great as they release their energy slowly, keeping you going for longer. Turn to Chapter 5 for some tasty recipes to try.

Carriers

If you're going on a long journey, or shopping, you'll need a safe way to carry things around. The good news is there are lots of relatively cheap options to choose from.

The best way is a basket on the front of your bike, or a rucksack on your back. These both keep your arms free. (Never try to carry a bag in your hand while cycling as it will throw you off balance or worse still, it could catch the spokes in your front wheel and throw you over the handlebars!) Some baskets are detachable so you can take them with you when you stop at a shop.

Many bikes have a rack above the back wheel, but make sure you use bungee cords to keep things attached securely.

WRAP THE BUNGEE CORD AROUND AND HOOK IT UNDER THE RACK TO SECURE.

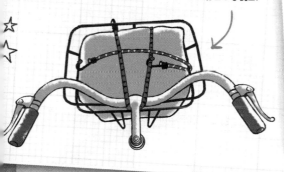

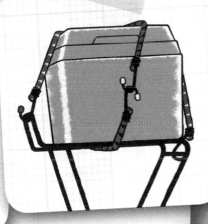

For really long trips you might want to think about getting panniers. These are bags that attach to the back of the bike, on each side of the wheel and can fit in changes of clothing and even a sleeping bag.

Stickers and Spoke Beads

There are all sorts of extras you can buy for your bike to bling it up. Stickers, or decals, are an easy way to make your bike stand out from the crowd. Spoke beads make a great noise, and so does our playing card engine! Turn to pages 130-131 to find out how to bling your bike up on the cheap. But remember, this really is an extra; it won't make you a better cyclist.

Fergus's
FASCINATING FACTS

In the olden days even racing clothes were odd. Cyclists wore wool, which was scratchy and got soggy when it rained. They switched to silk in the 1940s, which was much lighter and smoother. But man-made high-tech fabrics changed cycling and today people like Sir Chris wear jerseys and shorts made of material like Lycra. This is aerodynamic and wicks away sweat, keeping you cooler. Plus it can be printed with bright colours, which makes it look cooler too!

Nowadays girls wear the same as boys for riding a bike, but it wasn't always like that. Back in the 1800s, women wore long, billowy skirts all the time. But they're not great for cycling in, so they started to switch to bloomers – like puffy trousers that come just below the knee. Soon women started wearing these in everyday life too. So it's fair to say that the invention of bicycles changed the way women dressed in and out of the saddle.

Chris's
TOP TIPS

Before I head out anywhere, I tick off a checklist to make sure I'm prepared for anything. I check:

☐ MY TYRES ARE PUMPED UP
(turn to pages 62-63)

☐ MY HELMET'S FIRMLY ON MY NOGGIN

☐ MY BRAKES ARE WORKING
(turn to pages 60-61)

☐ MY LIGHTS ARE ON IF IT'S DARK OUT

☐ I'VE PACKED WATER AND SNACKS IF I'M GOING ANY DISTANCE

And last but not least, I make sure I'm **FIT, FOCUSED AND UP FOR ANYTHING!**

Fergus's
FASCINATING FACTS

In the 1830s a Scotsman, Kirkpatrick Macmillan, invented what many consider to be the first proper bicycle, with pedals used to propel it.

DAISY'S QUICKFIRE QUIZ

Time to test your biking knowledge. Answers are at the back of the book, but no peeking! If you're stuck, check back over the chapter – all the clues are there.

1 What's the other name for bike stickers?

2 What material did the earliest cyclists wear?

3 What are the two kinds of bike lock?

4 What are the lights called that work by pedal power?

5 Name two ways to let people know you're on the road.

ANSWERS ON PAGE 158.

Chapter 3

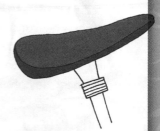

Basic Bike Maintenance

So now that you've chosen your bike, you need to know how to look after it. Just like our bodies, bikes need care and attention to keep them in tip-top condition. Looking after your bike is really important and it's all part of the fun of cycling.

This chapter will give you lots of useful tips and step-by-step instructions on how to maintain and service your bike, such as how to check your brakes, pump up your tyres, fix your chain if it comes off, clean your bike and lots more. For some people buying a second-hand bike and doing it up is their favourite part of being a cyclist, so we'll give you the basics on that too.

Finally, learning how to look after your pride and joy properly will mean it will last longer, ride better, and you'll have more fun!

How a Bike Works

✿ Chain reaction

The chain is used to link your pedals, cranks and front chainrings to the back wheel and the rear sprocket. When you push down on the pedals, this turns the cranks and chainrings and drags the chain round with it. This then pulls on the rear sprocket, which rotates the back wheel. Hey presto! You're moving forward!

✿ Taking it up a gear

Gears (or gear 'ratios') are made from the chainrings and sprockets on the bike. Using a lever on your handlebars to change gear changes the combination of chainrings and sprockets, making it easier or harder to pedal. When going uphill it's best to use a 'low' gear, by selecting a small chainring at the front and a big sprocket at the back. For downhill slopes or when you want to go fast on the flat, it's best to choose a 'high' gear – a big chainring on the front and a small sprocket on the back. It sounds complicated but with a bit of practice you will soon be an expert at changing gear.

✿ Slowing it down

Most bike brakes are simple rubber pads that work by squeezing against the rim of the wheel to slow it down when you pull on the brake levers. The right hand lever usually works the front brake and the left hand lever usually works the back. Always use both together. If you only use the front brake and pull too hard the back wheel can flip up, sending you flying over the handlebars. If you use only the back brake the wheel can sometimes skid, which can be fun, but will wear out your back tyre very quickly!

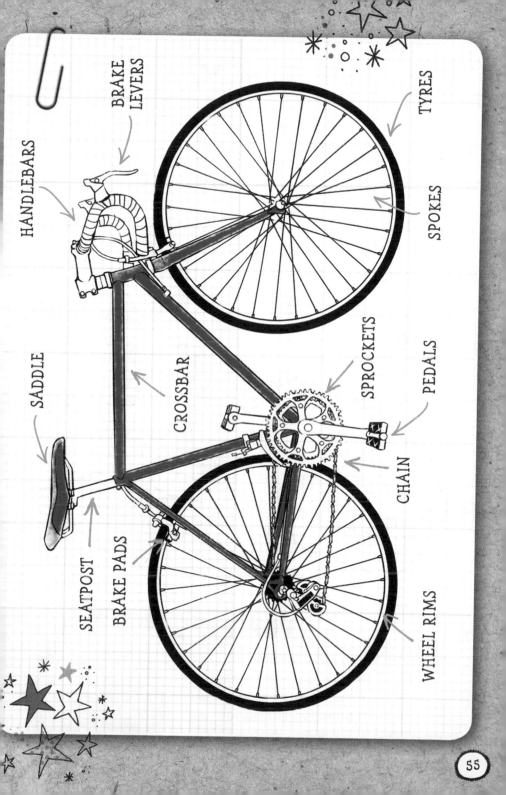

BRAKE
LEVERS

HANDLEBARS

TYRES

SPOKES

SADDLE

CROSSBAR

SPROCKETS

PEDALS

CHAIN

SEATPOST

BRAKE PADS

WHEEL RIMS

Caring For Your Bike

Your bike is bound to suffer a little wear and tear if you're riding it a lot and having fun, but there are ways to keep it roadworthy and looking its best. The easiest way is to look after it properly by following some simple rules and getting hold of a toolkit to help with maintenance.

⚙ Basic Tool Kit

To keep your bike in tip-top condition, you'll need:

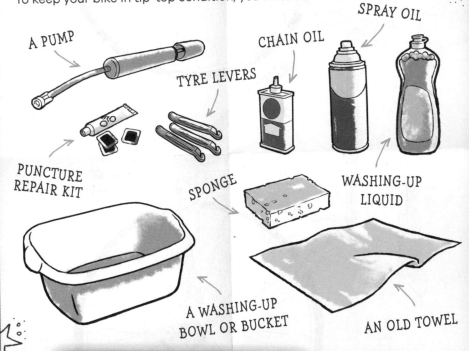

A PUMP

TYRE LEVERS

CHAIN OIL

SPRAY OIL

PUNCTURE REPAIR KIT

SPONGE

WASHING-UP LIQUID

A WASHING-UP BOWL OR BUCKET

AN OLD TOWEL

Chris's TOP TIPS

Before you do any maintenance or work on your bike, it's a good idea to get a grown-up to help you and make sure you are doing it right.

Daisy's
DOS AND DON'TS OF BIKE CARE

1. DO treat your bike kindly, and use a bike stand if you can. If you have to lay it down on the ground, never lie it on the right-hand side – this could damage the gear mechanisms.

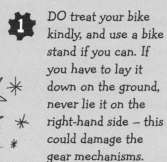 

2. DON'T drop it down on concrete or scrape it against a wall, that way it won't get too scratched.

3. DO keep it covered to stop it getting wet – water causes metal to rust. Keep it inside if you can, maybe in a garage or shed, or get a cheap waterproof cover to go over the bike in wet weather, or even a bike tent!

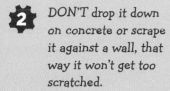 

4. DO make sure your bike's safe by always locking it at night.

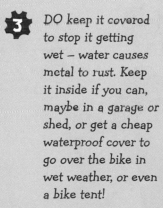 

Cleaning Your Bike

Cleaning your bike is important to prevent rust and will give you the chance to spot any problems before they cause damage. But it's also fun!

1. **Start with a bowl or bucket of warm, soapy water.**

2. **Use an old toothbrush or nail brush to get the worst of the mud off the tyres.**

3. **Use a sponge to clean the frame and wheels. (Don't use the brush on the frame or you could scratch it.)**

4. **Rinse off with a hose or a bucket of clean, cold water.**

5. **Use the old towel to dry the bike – remember you don't want to leave it too wet or rust can form.**

Oiling Your Bike

A spray of oil on the gears and chain keeps everything running smoothly. But don't use too much – it'll get on your clothing, and attract dirt, which slows everything down again.

⚙ OILING POINTS

CABLES

BRAKE LEVERS

BRAKE ARMS

DERAILLEURS

CHAIN

PEDALS

Don't ever get oil on the brake blocks or wheel rims, as they'll be too slippery to work!

Checking Your Brakes

Working brakes are crucial if you don't want to crash, so test them out every time you ride.

 1 Stand next to the bike and give the levers a squeeze to make sure the bike can't go forward.

 2 Next check the rubber brake pads. If they're getting worn down, then replace them.

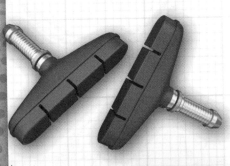

You can buy spare brake pads cheaply at any bike shop or online.

3 Whether you've replaced them or not, make sure the whole pad is touching the rim. It should be parallel or at a very slight angle (called 'toe-in'). If it's not touching it, or is too wonky, then undo the nut that holds it on and wiggle it into place. But make sure you tighten the nut again before you set off!

BRAKE PAD ALIGNED WITH RIM

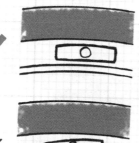

BRAKE PAD AND RIM PARALLEL

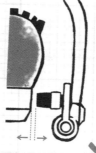

BRAKE PAD SLIGHT TOE ANGLE WITH RIM

Some bikes have a disc brake system, where the pads are attached to the hub of the wheel instead of to the rim of the tyres. They are less affected by mud and water and the pads last a long time, so can be a better system for some types of bike. However, they are harder to replace yourself, so take your bike to a good cycle shop to get help on maintaining them.

Fergus's
FASCINATING FACTS

The earliest bikes didn't have brakes at all. The only way to slow down was to use your feet, or fall off!

Pumping the Tyres

Even without a puncture, tyres can lose air and feel flat after a while. Flat tyres are more prone to punctures and will also slow you down, so before every ride check the tyres are firm enough.

1 Grip the tyre with your thumb and forefinger and give it a good squeeze. You shouldn't be able to squish it in more than a millimeter or so.

2 If it does squish easily, then take the valve cap off and put it aside in a safe place.

 3 Attach your pump and blow air in until it's fairly rigid, then screw the valve cap back on.

GO ONLINE TO WWW.FLYINGFERGUS.COM/ ONYOURBIKE FOR AN EXCLUSIVE BONUS VIDEO OF CHRIS CHECKING AND PUMPING UP A TYRE.

 4 While you're down there, check the tread on the tyres too – that's the patterned ridges that help the wheels grip the ground. If they're worn too flat, it could be time for new ones, or you risk slip-sliding around.

Fixing a Chain

Chains can and do come off, but putting them back on is easy (if a bit messy). All you have to do is stretch it back over the teeth on the chainring and sprocket. Get a grown-up to help you the first time, but soon you'll be an expert at doing it yourself if you follow these steps.

 Put your bike on its stand if it has one. If not then lay it down gently.

 Hook the chain onto the rear sprocket, then attach it to the top of the front chainring.

3 Turn the pedals forwards so the chain gets pulled around until it's sitting properly on both the chainring at the front and the sprocket at the back.

GO ONLINE TO WWW.FLYINGFERGUS.COM/ONYOURBIKE FOR AN EXCLUSIVE BONUS VIDEO OF HOW TO FIX A CHAIN!

Chris's TOP TIPS

If the chain keeps coming off it's worth getting your bike checked out at a bike shop. It may mean the chain has stretched or has a loose link, or the back wheel isn't correctly positioned.

Fergus's FASCINATING FACTS

Chains are a pretty recent invention, bike-wise. Before that the pedals were fixed to the front wheel of the bike, so when you pedalled you turned the wheel directly. That's why Penny Farthings had such big front wheels — it meant that one small turn of the pedals made a giant turn of the front wheel, getting the cyclist further, faster.

Mending a Puncture

A puncture happens when something sharp pricks a hole in a tyre's inner tube. Learning to repair a puncture yourself is one of the most useful lessons you can learn. Get a grown-up to help you the first few times.

1 First of all remove whatever's caused the puncture – maybe a thorn or a piece of glass – be very careful and wear gloves if you have them, because you don't want to hurt yourself while you're mending your bike!

2 Next, you need to take the wheel off and remove the inner tube. Unless you're lucky enough to have quick-release wheels, use a spanner to loosen the wheel nuts and then take off the valve cap and release any air that's left in the inner tube.

3 Use the tyre levers to work the tyre out from the wheel rim. To do that, hook one end of a lever under the rim and the other around a spoke. A few inches along, hook another under the rim and then run it round the inside of the rim pulling the tyre out as you go. Repeat this on the other side of the tyre.

4 Next you need to find the puncture hole in the inner tube. If you can't hear air hissing out, then put the tube in some water and look for bubbles.

5 Once you've found the hole (and got rid of any water in the tube), glue the patch in place from the puncture repair kit. It will either be sticky already, or there'll be a tube of glue included in the kit.

6 Last of all, you need to get the tyre and wheel back on. To do that, allow a small amount of air into the inner tube then put it back into the wheel, with the valve sticking through the hole. Tuck the tyre back into the wheel rim.

7 Finally, pump the tyre back up again.

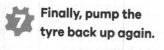

GO ONLINE TO WWW.FLYINGFERGUS.COM/ ONYOURBIKE FOR AN EXCLUSIVE BONUS VIDEO OF CHRIS MENDING A PUNCTURE.

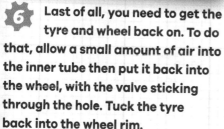

Second-hand Cycles

The same rules apply for buying a second-hand bike as buying a new one – first and foremost, make sure it's the right size for you (see pages 28-29), and adjust the handlebars and saddle if needed. With a second-hand bike, bear in mind it may have been ridden hard, or even been in an accident, so there are other things you'll need to look at before you buy, or once you've got the bike home.

GO ONLINE TO WWW.FLYINGFERGUS.COM/ONYOURBIKE FOR AN EXCLUSIVE BONUS VIDEO OF CHRIS INSPECTING A BIKE.

Grandpa Herc's
WISE ADVICE

⚙ Check the brake pads aren't too worn down (pages 60-61) – if they are, replace them.

⚙ Look at the tyres. If the tread is too worn down, then you can get replacements at most bike shops, although they may have to order them in for you.

⚙ The spokes should be straight and the wheels aligned – that means they're fixed upright and not wobbling or bending to one side. If they aren't properly aligned, then take the bike to a repair shop to get the wheel straightened. If they can't straighten it easily, you may need a new one.

⚙ Don't be disheartened if the bike's a bit rusty or the paintwork's scratched. That's easily fixed with a lick of paint. Rub down the rust with wire wool (wear gloves or get a grown-up to help you with that bit) and give it a coat of rust prevention paint. Then you can paint the whole bike using any colour, or combination of colours you like. The best paint to use is specialist metal or car paint. Spray will give a smoother surface, but get a grown-up to do that for you as it can be messy and give off smelly fumes.

Chris's TOP TIPS

However tempting it might be, don't clean your bike on the kitchen table unless you get permission. Like Fergus, I learned the hard way from my mum that bike oil and baking don't mix!

As soon as you notice something feeling odd with your bike when you are riding it, stop and check to see if there is a problem, before you have an accident!

DAISY'S QUICKFIRE QUIZ

- →

Time to test your biking knowledge.
Answers are at the back of the book,
but no peeking! If you're stuck, check back
over the chapter – all the clues are there.

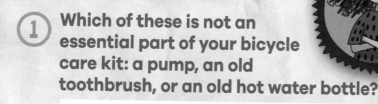

1 Which of these is not an essential part of your bicycle care kit: a pump, an old toothbrush, or an old hot water bottle?

2 What are the toothed discs on the back wheel called that the chain attaches to?

3 What are two ways you can find the puncture in an inner tube?

4 If a chain keeps falling off should you fix it yourself or go to a repair shop?

5 How much of the brake block should touch the wheel rim when the brake is on: all of it, half of it, one tip of it?

ANSWERS ON PAGE 158.

GIVE WAY

THE HIGHWAY CODE

AA
HIGHWAY CODE
ESSENTIAL FOR ALL DRIVERS

Fully updated and complete

Plus TAKING YOUR TEST
what to expect

Updated RULES for the
ROAD for all drivers

Key information for ALL
ROAD USERS including
cyclists and motorcyclists

Chapter 4

ENJOYING RACING DOWNHILL ON MY ROAD BIKE

Safety First

Cycling should be fun first and foremost, but it's really important for you to be safe in the saddle and aware of your surroundings.

If you're putting yourself or others in danger, then no one's going to enjoy the ride. It doesn't matter where you are about to cycle, safety always starts with helmet and bike checks, and when you're out on the road there are some other important things you need to think about too. This chapter will give you tips about staying safe and teach you the rules of the road.

When I'm out and about on my bike, there's one important motto I always stick to: be polite. That means watching out for pedestrians (people crossing the road on foot) and all other road users (some of them are cyclists too!)

Before You Set Off

Before you even get on your bike, you'll need to know where you're going! Choose a route that's going to be fun, but as safe as possible.

⚙ Choosing a route

If you don't know the way off by heart then take a map with you in case you get lost. You can buy special map pouches to keep it round your neck, or pop it in your rucksack or basket.

If you can, stick to parks or cycle paths – it's always more fun to ride where there's less traffic.

There are miles and miles of special cycle paths all over the country, all part of the National Cycle Network. You can find the paths near you by looking at your local Ordnance Survey maps. The National Trust also lists cycle routes on its website, and so does Sustrans (see page 159 for useful web links). Many towns and cities have specialised cycle parks too. You can check on the Flying Fergus website for an up-to-date list.

Pick quieter residential streets or 'B' roads if you can. 'A' roads or 'trunk' roads tend to be busier, and you should never ever try to cycle on a motorway – it's against the law for good reason.

✿ Ready to Ride

So you're all set to go, with a route picked.
But don't forget to check your bike before
you start out on your adventure. Tick off the
checklist over the page each time you ride.
After a while, you'll know it off by heart.

Calamity's
CRITICAL CHECKLIST

1 Are you wearing your helmet and does it still fit properly? (See pages 36-37)

2 Is your clothing right for cycling and for the weather? Make sure it's bright and light, so you can be easily seen easily. (See page 38)

3 Have you packed water and snacks? (Grab some tasty recipes from chapter 5)

4 Are your tyres pumped up? (See pages 62-63)

5 Are the brakes, bell and lights on your bike working? (See pages 60-61)

6 Have you told someone where you're going and when you'll be back again? Never ride off without letting someone know where you're going to. A mobile phone can be handy too, if you have one.

Fergus's
FASCINATING FACTS

No one thought to make a bicycle small enough for children until the 1920s – over 100 years after the first bicycle was invented! Luckily now we get almost as much choice as grown-ups and there are races and events just for us too.

Fergus and Chimp's 10 RULES OF THE ROAD

1 DO look all around you for traffic before you pull out, and DON'T wear headphones on a cycle ride. Your most important pieces of equipment are your eyes and ears, so remember to use them at all times.

2 DON'T start pedalling until you're sure the road is safe and clear.

3 DO check ahead for potential hazards – like pedestrians, or dips in the road, which are called pot holes.

4 DON'T ride through icky things like banana skins and dog poo!

5 DO keep both hands on the handlebars unless you need to signal left or right. That way you're less likely to wobble if you hit a pot hole or piece of litter.

6 DO be polite to other road users – that means pedestrians as well as other cyclists and drivers too. The nicer you are to them, the nicer they're likely to be to you. They might even catch the cycling bug when they see how much fun you're having.

7 DON'T try to undertake, or ride up the inside of a line of traffic. It's dangerous – if you skid you could crash into a car, and you never know when a driver might swerve to the left. Traffic jams can be annoying but it's not worth risking your neck.

8 DO let other road users know where you're going and what you're doing. If you're turning left or right or slowing down use the special hand signals just for cyclists (turn the page to find out more).

TURNING LEFT   TURNING RIGHT

9 DON'T get too close to parked cars. Always be ready to brake in case someone opens a car door in your path. Give yourself room so that if this happens you won't have to swerve into traffic that's behind you.

10 DO use a cycle track if there is one, but DON'T ride on the pavement. If a junction looks difficult, safety comes first and you should dismount and walk your bike across as a pedestrian.

LOOK OUT FOR THE CYCLE PATH SIGN, AND BE AWARE OF PEDESTRIANS.

How to Signal

Bikes don't have indicators and brake lights like cars, so cyclists use their arms to let other road users know what they're up to.

✿ Turning right

To turn right, stick your right arm out straight. Once you've turned the corner you can put both hands back on the handlebars.

BE AWARE OF OTHER TRAFFIC AND MAKE SURE IT'S CLEAR TO GO BEFORE YOU START THE TURN.

⚙ Turning left

**To turn left, do the same
on the other side.**

Practise in your garden first
or in the park so you can be sure you
can balance easily when cycling with
one hand. See pages 124-5 for tips.

The Highway Code

As well as being safe, and being polite, there are real rules of the road that we all have to follow, whether we're on two legs, two wheels or in a car. Together, they're called the Highway Code and you can find a copy in all bookshops and online too. The code tells you all about things like speed limits, where you can and can't go on a bike and what all the traffic signs mean.

Fergus's FASCINATING FACTS

The Highway Code is one of the best-selling books of all time. It was first published in 1931, when cars began to become popular, and now hundreds of thousands of copies are snapped up each year and it saves thousands of lives.

Traffic signs

Traffic signs generally come in three shapes.

CIRCLES GIVE ORDERS　　**TRIANGLES GIVE WARNINGS**　　**RECTANGLES GIVE INFORMATION**

 Blue circles generally give an instruction about what to do, such as 'turn left' or indicate a route available only to particular classes of traffic, e.g. buses and cycles only.

 Red rings or circles tell you what you must not do, e.g. you must not exceed 30mph.

Know Your TRAFFIC SIGNS
Official Edition

There are a few exceptions to the shape and colour rules, to give certain signs greater prominence. Examples are the "STOP" and "GIVE WAY" signs.

83

The Signs You Need to Know

Some of the most important traffic signs are:

This means that you need to stop and let other road users go first.

This NO ENTRY sign means you can't cycle down this road – either it's a one-way street or for pedestrians only – so you'll need to get off your bike and walk.

 **Speed**

You're not likely to be breaking the speed limit, but it's good to know that if there are streetlights, then the limit is likely to be 30 miles per hour or less. If there are no street lights, then it's 60mph – the national speed limit on a single carriageway.

You might see this sign if you're out in a hilly area. Keep an eye out, as there may already be rocks in the road.

No, this isn't a warning about flying motorbikes, it means no motorbikes or cars are allowed, but you are allowed to ride your bike here.

Fergus's
FASCINATING FACTS

The sign for 'national speed limit' looks like this. It's designed that way because it's telling us there are no more street lights!

Special Signs for Cyclists

Keep an eye out for the signs that are meant just for people like you. They're usually blue with white pictures on, like these ones.

This sign means that this part of the road is a special lane just for cycles, so cars can't go in it. But keep an eye out – not everyone follows the rules as well as you will.

Unlike cars, bikes are allowed to use the bus lane. But be careful when you do and never try to sneak up the inside of a bus. It's hard for drivers to see you in their mirrors and they might be just about to pull over to a stop.

This sign has got a red ring round it, meaning it's something you mustn't do. This one means you can't go down here on a bike. You'll have to find a different route or get off and walk.

Some signs are painted on the road itself. The one in the picture above means that this part of the road is a cycle lane.

Chris's TOP TIPS

Learning all the traffic signs can be fun – why not set your friends a quiz so you can all learn together?

Accidents Happen

Everyone takes a tumble from time to time – even professional cyclists can come a cropper! When you do fall off, check yourself and your bike for damage, and if everything's working fine, dust yourself off and get back in the saddle as soon as you can.

Chris's TOP TIPS

I've lost count of the number of times I've fallen off – but all that's hurt usually is my pride! To avoid accidents in the first place, always try to think and look ahead. And it's a good idea to have a plaster or two in a small First Aid kit if you're out on a long ride.

Fergus's
FASCINATING FACTS

In the 1990s Scottish cyclist Graeme Obree became world champion and broke records on a bike that he designed and built himself using bits of scrap metal and parts from a washing machine!

DAISY'S QUICKFIRE QUIZ

Time to test your biking knowledge.
Answers are at the back of the book,
but no peeking! If you're stuck, check back
over the chapter – all the clues are there.

1  **What does this road sign mean?**

2 **When was the Highway Code first published?**

3 **If you want to turn right, how do you let other road users know what you're going to do?**

4 **What are holes in the road called?**

5 **If you fall off, should you get back in the saddle, or walk home?**

ANSWERS ON PAGE 158.

Chapter 5

ON THE OLYMPIC MEDAL WINNERS' PODIUM. BEING IN TOP SHAPE WAS CRUCIAL TO MY SUCCESS.

Keeping Cycling Fit

Cycling isn't just fun, it's good for you too – that's why grown-ups are so keen to get you in the saddle.

To be a top cyclist, you need to be super fit and strong, and follow special exercise regimes and diets. But even if you're never going to race for a career, like me, every cyclist needs to think about what they eat and keep their body in good condition, to get the most from their time on their bikes.

So this chapter will show you some exercises for your whole family to try out at home, as well as recipes for some of my favourite food to keep me going on longer rides.

And who knows – if you work really hard and stick at it, maybe you could eventually become a top Olympic cyclist too.

Exercising Right

Cycling is one of the easiest and most enjoyable ways to get fit and stay fit. Even an hour a week racing round the park will make a big difference to how well your body works.

But becoming a better cyclist starts even before you get in the saddle, with exercise. Top cyclists can spend hours a day in the gym, making sure their bodies are in tip-top shape. You don't need loads of time or special machines and weights to make sure you're bike-fit though. Why not try out some of our easy exercises at home? All you'll need is some space in the front room or garden, and some loose clothes.

IN SHAPE AND ON MY BIKE READY FOR THE 2012 WORLD TRACK CHAMPIONSHIPS

Chris's TOP TIPS

Cycling is no different to other hobbies like playing the piano or drawing or doing keepie-uppies with a football – it takes practice to get better. If I didn't train hard I wouldn't be a champion, I'd just be a bloke with a fancy bike.

Fergus's
FASCINATING FACTS

Being fit isn't just good for your body, it's good for your mind too. There's loads of evidence that the fitter you are, the better you concentrate and the better your brain can function. So if you want to get ahead at school, get on your bike!

Warming Up and Down

Muscles work best when they've been allowed to warm up first, so they're nice and stretchy. You're also less likely to injure yourself. So before you get on your bike do some simple stretches to get your body ready to go. And if you can find the time to repeat them at the end of the ride, even better. That way your muscles won't stiffen up so easily afterwards. Remember as well to listen to your own body – if you've got an injury or something doesn't feel right, please see your doctor first to get everything checked out before doing any exercises.

✿ Side stretch

Stand with your feet apart and your hands on your hips. Lift your right arm up straight and bend at the waist towards the left. Repeat on the other side and then start again. Do the exercise ten times each side in total. Each time try to bend a bit further.

✿ Neck stretch

Sitting in one position in the saddle for a long time can give you a stiff neck, so stretch yours out before you start. Drop your head forward so your chin meets your chest, then lift your head up again. Next stretch your neck from side to side.. That will help loosen your shoulders out too. Do this a few times until you feel nicely stretched.

✿ Leg stretches

Stand with your legs apart. Bend your right knee to the side so that it's above your toes. Repeat on the left and then do the whole exercise again ten times. Try moving your feet a little further apart each time to really stretch your inner thighs.

LISTEN TO YOUR BODY. IF IT HURTS, STOP!

Building Strength

Cycling works on three kinds of leg muscle:

 1 Your gluteus maximus (your backside)

 2 Your quadriceps (your upper thighs)

 3 Your gastrocnemius and soleus (your calf muscles)

The warm-up leg stretches will help build some strength in your upper thighs, but squats can really help too, as well as work on the old gluteus maximus.

☼ Basic squat

Stand with your feet slightly apart and your arms straight out in front of you. Then crouch down steadily, but keep your head facing forward and your back straight. Stand up again slowly, keeping your back straight still, using your thigh and bottom muscles to push you up. Repeat this ten times.

☼ Wall squat

Stand with your back flat against a smooth wall and slowly lower yourself until your thighs are parallel to the floor. Your knees should be at right angles. Try to hold this position for as long as possible. It'll be easy at first, but it gets tiring very quickly. For a fun challenge, why not do it with your friends (or family!) to see who can hold it for the longest time.

Building Stamina

There's one other major muscle that needs to be in tip-top shape for cycling: your heart!

Your heart is constantly pumping oxygen round your body in your blood. And when you're exercising, it has to beat even faster as your leg muscles need more and more oxygen to get up to speed, and it needs to be able to do that for a long time – that's what we call 'stamina' or 'endurance'.

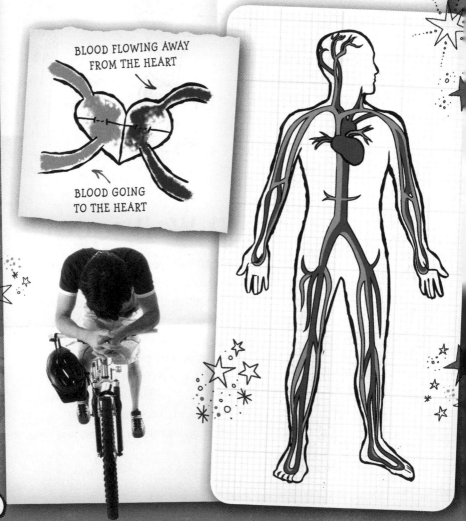

BLOOD FLOWING AWAY
FROM THE HEART

BLOOD GOING
TO THE HEART

To build stamina you need to do the kind of exercise that makes you out of breath – so cycling, running around or even swimming.

If you can do twenty minutes of one of those, three times a week (it doesn't have to be the same one each time) you're well on your way to building up the stamina your heart needs to keep you in the saddle for longer.

Chris's TOP TIPS

Even the best cyclists in the world had to start somewhere, so don't be disheartened with your fitness if it takes a while to see improvements.

Building Up Speed

The stronger your legs are and the more stamina you have the quicker you'll go. But how fast you can cycle isn't just down to your muscles; speed is affected by other forces too.

⚙ Gravity

Gravity is the invisible force, a bit like magnetism, which pulls us towards the ground – especially important if we fall off!

⚙ Friction

Friction, which is what happens when two things rub together, also slows us down. So make sure your chain and sprockets are well oiled so they turn as smoothly as possible, and that the brake blocks aren't rubbing against the wheels.

⚙ Air Resistance

Air resistance is another form of friction. We notice it most when riding into a headwind, but it affects us even when there is no wind at all. You can reduce air resistance by wearing close-fitting clothing, leaning low over the handlebars, and keeping your elbows in. This helps us to 'cut through' the air more easily and move along faster without having to pedal any harder.

Fergus's
FASCINATING FACTS

You can save up to a third of your energy by riding in someone else's slipstream, (that means behind them). That way you don't have the same force of air or wind against you slowing you down.

AIR RESISTANCE

GRAVITY
(RIDER AND BIKE)

FRICTION

Fergus's
FASCINATING FACTS

Ever wondered why racers wear helmets shaped like teardrops? That way the air slips over the surface, meaning they can keep their speed up more easily.

Eating Right

When you're out on your bike you burn off massive amounts of energy. At a good speed that can be up to 650 calories an hour – that's the amount of energy in six whole bananas, or thirteen apples.

But just because you're burning off all that energy, it doesn't mean you can eat loads of junk food. The better the food you put in your body, the more you'll get out of your body in terms of fitness.

Top athletes have to eat really well, and follow special diets before races that give them all the nutrients they need. But you can make a big difference by making sure you're eating right at home. Make sure you always eat balanced meals – that means having a good mixture of protein, carbohydrates and veg every day. If you're a fan of fishfingers like Fergus, eat them with peas and potatoes too and you've got all three food groups covered.

Obviously when you're out on your bike you can't carry around a pocketful of rice, but you can take some snacks with you on a long ride. But be wise about what you choose. Some snacks are full of sugar – that will give you an instant hit of energy but won't sustain you over a longer ride. Try out some of the great recipes in the next few pages for healthy, delicious snacks – and they're easy to carry too.

MAKE SURE YOU GET A GROWN-UP TO HELP WITH HANDLING OVENS AND HOT TINS.

- Protein helps your muscles grow and keeps them in prime condition – protein is in meat, fish, dairy products like milk and cheese, soya, nuts, and pulses like lentils and beans.

- Fruit and veg contain vitamins – so make sure you get at least five portions a day, and if you can aim for ten, then you're on your way to serious cycle fitness.

- Carbohydrates like rice, potatoes and pasta will keep you going, especially before and during a long ride. They may be last in the list, but you won't get far without them!

Daisy's DAILY DIET

VEGETABLES

CARBOHYDRATES

LIQUID

PROTEIN

FRUIT

DAIRY

Chris's TOP TIPS

Stick to carbs that release their energy slowly. A banana is a great ready-wrapped snack for when you're out on the bike, or you can buy things like oat bars or pack up a homemade flapjack.

Fergus's Fave Fruity Flapjacks

Oats are a great source of slow-release energy, and make up a bit for the butter and sugar that's in these delicious squares.

⚙ What you'll need

175g butter

175g golden caster sugar

175g golden syrup

350g porridge oats

A handful of raisins, chopped dried apricots or sultanas

20cm by 20cm baking tin or equivalent

Greaseproof paper

A big saucepan

A wooden spoon

HOW TO DO IT

① Set the oven to 150°C (300°F / gas mark 2).

② Cut the greaseproof paper to the right size and line your tin.

③ Melt the butter in a big saucepan on the hob (use a low heat or the butter will start to sizzle).

④ Add the sugar and golden syrup and stir until dissolved.

⑤ Take the pan off the heat and add the oats and fruit. Stir well – it will be sticky!

⑥ Pack the mixture into the baking tin and squish down.

⑦ Bake for 35-40 minutes.

⑧ Take the tin out of the oven and leave to cool for 15 minutes.

⑨ Turn the flapjack out and cut into squares (the size is up to you).

⑩ Try not to scoff them all at once!

ASK A GROWN-UP FOR HELP WITH HOT OVENS, AND DON'T FORGET YOUR OVEN GLOVES!

You can leave the fruit out if you're not keen, or even swap it with dark chocolate chips (much better for you than milk chocolate ones, and just as delicious).

Chimp's Cheesetastic Scones

Not all of us have a sweet tooth, so how about some cheesy scones for when you're out on the road? You can eat them plain, or sliced and spread with your favourite topping. Chimp loves butter and Marmite!

☼ What you'll need

250g self-raising flour

50g cold butter, chopped into small cubes

75g grated cheese (Cheddar is a good one)

125ml milk

A big baking tray

A large bowl

A sieve

Greaseproof paper

A round pastry cutter

A rolling pin

HOW TO DO IT

1. Preheat the oven to 220°C (425°F / gas mark 7)

2. Grease the baking tray and cut the greaseproof paper to the right size then line the tray.

3. Sieve the flour into the bowl.

4. Add the butter and using the tips of your fingers, rub it into the flour until it looks like breadcrumbs. Stir in the cheese.

5. Make a well in the middle of the mixture and pour in most of the milk – keep a little bit back.

6. Mix together until it's a squidgy dough. If it's a bit dry, you can add a bit more milk. If it's too wet, add a little more flour.

7. Sprinkle flour over the kitchen counter and then roll out the dough with your rolling pin until it's about 2cm thick.

8. Cut out the scone shapes and pop on the tray, then reshape any leftover dough and reroll. Cut out until you can't make any more.

9. Brush the tops of the scones with the leftover milk (this makes them shiny), and bake in the oven for 12-15 minutes or until golden-brown.

10. Pop on a cooling rack – if you can resist eating one fresh from the oven!

ASK A GROWN-UP FOR HELP WITH HOT OVENS, AND DON'T FORGET YOUR OVEN GLOVES!

If you're not a fan of cheese, you can turn these into fruit scones by swapping the cheese for currants or sultanas.

Daisy's Beast Banana Bread

Bananas are brilliant for you, but taste even better in this yummy loaf cake that's bursting with flavour. Eat a slice on its own or you could toast it for breakfast and spread with Daisy's favourite – peanut butter and chocolate spread!

✿ What you'll need

115g butter

115g light brown sugar

2 beaten eggs

4 mashed ripe bananas
(the squidgier the better)

250g plain flour

1 tsp bicarbonate of soda

A pinch of salt

A 2lb (23cm x 13cm) loaf tin

Greaseproof paper or
a loaf tin liner

A big bowl

A wooden spoon

A metal skewer

HOW TO DO IT

1. Preheat the oven to 180°C (350°F / gas mark 4) and line the loaf tin.

2. In a big bowl, cream together the butter and sugar.

3. Add the eggs and bananas (the mixture will be quite sloppy by now).

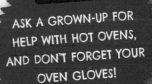

ASK A GROWN-UP FOR HELP WITH HOT OVENS, AND DON'T FORGET YOUR OVEN GLOVES!

4. Stir in the flour, salt and bicarbonate of soda. Don't worry if it looks a bit lumpy!

5. Pour into the loaf tin and bake for one hour.

6. Check it's cooked by sticking a skewer into the middle of the loaf. It should come out cleanish. If there's sloppy mixture stuck to it, the bread isn't done yet so give it another five minutes and check again.

7. When the skewer comes out clean, remove from the oven and leave to cool in the tin for quarter of an hour, then turn out onto a cooling rack.

You can add chopped walnuts to this for some extra protein, or dark chocolate chips for a chocotastic kick.

Minnie's Maxi Muffins

More oats and bananas, this time in a very moreish muffin. And these tasty cakes are packed with blueberries too, making them a perfect pre-ride breakfast or on-the-go snack.

⚙ What you'll need

200g plain flour

200g porridge oats

75g golden caster sugar

3tsp baking powder

2 mashed ripe bananas

2 beaten eggs

3 tbsp oil (sunflower or vegetable)

250ml milk

100g blueberries

A 12-hole muffin tin and cases

A big bowl

A wooden spoon

ASK A GROWN-UP FO
HELP WITH HOT OVE
AND DON'T FORGET Y
OVEN GLOVES!

HOW TO DO IT

① Preheat the oven to 200°C (400°F / gas mark 6) and pop the muffin cases in the tin.

② In a big bowl, mix the flour, oats, sugar and baking powder.

③ Make a well in the middle and add the bananas, eggs, oil and milk. Mix it together until it's nice and sloppy.

④ Stir in the blueberries.

⑤ Pour into the muffin cases and bake for 25 minutes. They should be puffy and golden on top.

⑥ Cool on a rack.

You can add all sorts of things to these muffins. Chopped walnuts or dark chocolate chips work really well instead of blueberries. Or swap some of the oats for dessicated coconut.

Fergus's
FASCINATING FACTS

Velo means 'bicycle' in French. The first bicycle ever made was called a Velocipede, and one of the clubs I've raced against is called the Velociraptors!

Fergus's
FASCINATING FACTS

There are more than one billion bicycles in the world, with half a billion in China alone. But the Dutch are keen cyclists too – nearly all adults in Holland own a bike. Do the rest of your family own one? If not, maybe you could encourage them to saddle up too!

DAISY'S QUICKFIRE QUIZ

Time to test your biking knowledge.
Answers are at the back of the book,
but no peeking! If you're stuck, check back
over the chapter – all the clues are there.

1 What's the more
common name for your
gluteus maximus muscle?

2 How many calories an hour can cycling burn?

3 Fish, meat and eggs are all sources of what?

4 What's the most important muscle
for stamina?

5 The soleus is a muscle in which part of the leg:
thigh, calf or bottom?

ANSWERS ON PAGE 158.

Chapter 6

Top Tricks and Fun Stuff

I may be known for my races on the velodrome, but my first cycling love was BMX. All I wanted to do was to get both wheels off the ground and fly like the kids in the film E.T.

Now I'm not necessarily going to recommend you copy what I did (I came a cropper many times when I flew off my home-made ramp!) but this chapter will give you some ideas on tricks you can try out at home or, better, in the cycle park. Remember to stay safe while you practise – it can take some time to perfect your skills, so don't rush things and get the basics right before you try the more difficult jumps and tricks.

And there's other fun stuff too: from races and competition ideas to cheap ways to bling up your bike.

WEARING BLUE AND YELLOW ON
THE BMX STARTING BLOCKS

Trying Out Tricks

There are a few rules you need to follow when you're trying out tricks. Whether you're perfecting your wheelies, working on your balance for no-hands cycling to impress your friends or being the best at bunny hops, you can't have fun unless you're realistic about your skills. That means don't do too much too soon. Practice makes perfect but remember to take it slow and steady and learn at a pace that's sensible.

BUILDING AN OBSTACLE COURSE AGED SIX (NOTE THE STYLISH CAP MY MUM EMBROIDERED "BMX" ON)

TAKING AIR AGED ELEVEN

Minnie's THREE TIPS FOR TOP TRICKS

1. Don't do anything unless you're confident. If you're nervous, you'll wobble, and that's when you're likely to take a tumble.

2. Stay safe. So wear your helmet, of course, but pop on pads too, and make sure you're on soft ground like grass.

3. Have someone with you in case you do come a cropper. Even if you don't, it's great to have an audience!

Chris's TOP TIPS

Get your balance right and you'll find doing tricks much easier. The golden rule for balancing and control on a bike is to look where you want to go, and not look at the objects you are trying to avoid.

Wheelies

Wheelies are a great way to impress your mates, and one of the easiest tricks to learn. If you keep practising, you'll be able to get a bit higher, and go a bit further each time.

1 Make sure you're in a low gear and you have both hands on the handlebars, and your hand covering the back brake lever.

2 When you're steady, lean back so your weight is over the back wheel.

3 Yank up hard on the handlebars at the same time as pushing down on the pedals. The front wheel should lift off the ground.

4 To get back on the ground, lean forward and let the wheel drop, or gently pull the back brake lever.

Bunny Hops

Bunny hops are wheelies taken up a level, so make sure you've perfected those first.

1 Lift your weight off the seat, stand on the pedals and make sure your elbows and knees are ready to be 'springy'.

2 Pull hard on the handlebars at the same time as lifting up with your legs into a wheelie.

3 The back wheel should lift up too if you get the timing exactly right.

4 Keep your knees and elbows loose as you land both wheels back down together.

Bunny hops take a lot of practice to get right, but once you've cracked them it's a great skill to have, as it allows you to hop over obstacles once you get stronger and more confident.

No-Hands Cycling

Cycling is all about balance – that's why one of the best ways to learn how to ride is on a balance bike. Stabilisers trick you into thinking you're steady when really they're doing the balancing for you. If you want to ride without using your hands you'll need to take balancing up a level and be able to find and refind your centre of gravity.

ALWAYS DO THIS AWAY FROM BUSY AREAS AND NEVER DO IT ON A PUBLIC ROAD.

1 Ride along for a few metres at a steady speed – not too slow or you'll wobble, not too fast or you could swerve and fall off.

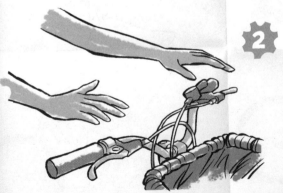

2 When you feel ready, lift one hand off the handlebars – only by about ten centimetres. Then, gently lift the other hand for a second or so. Don't jerk, or this will throw you off balance.

3 Keep pedalling smoothly and looking straight ahead in the direction you want to go. As soon as you feel yourself start to wobble, put your hands back on the handlebars.

4 Build up the amount of time you can cycle no-handed by a second each time until you're confident to ride for a good 20 metres. And move your hands further away from the handlebars as well.

Eventually you should be able to balance with both your hands by your sides.

You'll need a nice smooth hard surface with no obstacles nearby – this is one trick you can't perfect on grass, unless it's really level.

Race Against Your Mates

Racing games are a great way of building up speed and endurance. But don't take it too seriously – it's not all about winning. Give it your all, but most importantly, HAVE FUN!

⚙ Time Trial

Why not set up one of the easiest races of all – a time trial. That's when you each race around a set distance against the clock.

Usually time trials on the road are at least 10 kilometres long, but you can make yours as long or short as you want. To get started you'll need a track – you don't need any special surface, your local park will do.

- ⚙ **Plot out a route using markers like trees, or benches, or your own jackets. But be careful to keep out of the way of other people playing!**

- ⚙ **Take turns to go round while one of you times the other. See who's fastest, and see if you can build up your speed with each go.**

MY FIRST BRITISH NATIONAL TRACK CHAMPIONSHIPS, AGED SIXTEEN. RIDING IN THE KILO (IN DUNEDIN CYCLING CLUB COLOURS).

⚙ Pursuit

This is a race between two cyclists each trying to catch up with the other.

Mark out a track and have two of you start at opposite sides, but going in the same direction. See which one of you can gain the most ground on the other over a set time.

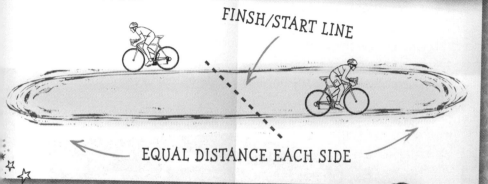

FINSH/START LINE

EQUAL DISTANCE EACH SIDE

Chris's TOP TIPS

Remember, winning isn't everything. Being a real champion doesn't mean coming first past the post every time, it means learning from the times you don't win. It's not cool to be a bad winner either. So don't show-off when you come in first and if you're not as fast as your friends, don't get upset, get some practice in! (But not before giving them a pat on the back! Your teammates are your friends, don't take your frustration out on them.)

⚙ Devil Take the Hindmost

This is a knock-out race, where the last across the line each lap loses their place. Keep going until there's only two of you left, then it's down to a straight head-to-head race to the finish line.

⚙ Slow Bicycle Race

It's fun to go fast on a bike, but have you ever tried to go as slow as possible? This is another great way to practise your balancing skills.

Get some friends together and set up a short track, preferably on grass. Use chalk or paint to mark a finish line – this is one race where every inch counts so posts won't work. Once the whistle has blown or the bell been dinged, see who can take the longest time possible to get across the finish line without falling off.

Make sure you have lots of space around each of you, and wear your helmet AND pads for this one if you've got them.

⚙ Slalom

If you've got a big garden, or live near a park, then a slalom is great fun as well as being good for improving your control.

Set up a line of at least five posts or cones wide apart, then take turns to cycle in and out of them. Once you've all managed them, move the posts closer together and go again.

Chris's TOP TIPS

If you don't have posts or cones for a slalom, then buckets or even jumpers will do! (But check with a grown-up first – you don't want to ruin your mum's best cardi with muddy wheelmarks!)

Bling Up Your Bike

There are all sorts of ways to make your bike stand out and express your personality.

⚙ Name your bike

Racehorses have cool names, so why shouldn't bicycles?

Think up a great name for your bike, then paint it on the chain guard or down tube with enamel pens, or use letter stickers.

TRY OUT YOUR OWN NAMES & DESIGNS HERE

You can buy spoke beads in bike shops, and decal stickers to decorate the frame with.

✿ Playing card engine

YOU'LL NEED:

✿ **A playing card**

✿ **A clothes peg or masking tape**

HOW TO DO IT:

Using the clothes peg or masking tape, fix the playing card to the back frame of the bike so that the card rests against the spokes. When you start pedaling, the card will slap against the wheel making a sound like a motorbike!

CLACK! CLACK! CLACK! CLACK! CLACK! CLACK! CLACK! CLACK! CLACK! CLACK! CLACK! CLACK! CLACK! CLACK! CLACK!

Grandpa Herc's
WISE ADVICE

Once you've finished, get a grown-up to check your work. Anything that could get caught in the spokes or tangled in your legs is a big no-no!

Set up a Cycling Club

Lots of areas have cycling clubs, but if there isn't one near you, then why not team up with your friends and start your very own? It doesn't take a lot of equipment or a fancy track. All you really need are bikes and some enthusiasm.

Your first job will be to come up with a cool name. How about The Sprocket Grinders, the Gear Changers, or the Dirt Eaters? I'm sure you can think of a better name than those!

Then set up some good games and challenges. Try the ones in this chapter or come up with some of your own – as long as they're safe!

RACE ACTION AGED TEN

Fergus's
FASCINATING FACTS

The first BMX races were held on big motocross tracks. Nowadays there are loads of purpose-built courses, designed to get the most out of the bikes and riders.

DAISY'S QUICKFIRE QUIZ

Time to test your biking knowledge.
Answers are at the back of the book,
but no peeking! If you're stuck, check back
over the chapter – all the clues are there.

1 A race in and out of
cones or posts
is called a what?

2 What trick do you need to perfect
before you try a bunny hop?

3 What's the most important thing
to perfect in no-hands cycling?

4 What kind of race is a
Devil Take the Hindmost?

5 What's the first job of a cycling club?

ANSWERS ON PAGE 158.

Chapter 7

Cycle Log

Now I've done my bit, and told you all my tips and tricks, it's over to you!

This is the part of the book where you can record your best cycle times and your favourite routes, as well as write down any adventures you have out on your bike.

Once you're back home you can find out more at www.flyingfergus.co.uk/onyourbike. Join the exclusive Flying Fergus Fan Club and as well as finding out more about my pals Fergus, Daisy and the team, I'll be adding new ideas and competitions, as well as lists of great places to ride, and learn about cycling.

Believe me – every ride can be an adventure! So have fun out there.

GETTING OUT ON THE ROAD WITH SOME FRIENDS, YOUNG AND OLD.

Out and About

The best thing about cycling is being in the open air. Make the most of it and remember where you went and what you did with these ideas.

✿ Logging your progress

Keep a log of all your cycle rides. Make a note of the date, the weather, where you went from and to, how long it took, and how far you travelled (you can find that out using the internet, a phone app, or a good old-fashioned map). There are Log Book pages to fill in at the end of the book to get you started.

✿ Routes to try out

There are loads of places you can go to find cycle routes near you. Turn to page 159 to get all the information on where to find ideas or get out your local maps and write down some rides you want to do. Then tick them off when you've tried them out. Include details of what makes them good, or where the problems are – like heavy traffic, or skiddy surfaces.

✿ Perfect your stunts

What stunts have you learned? Record your attempts in the Stunt Record at the back of the book. If you learn to rockwalk or manual like a pro, then write it down, along with the date.

WHEN	START	FINISH	WHERE I WENT	TOTAL DISTANCE	WHAT HAPPENED
Mon 1/6/2016	4.00pm	4.25pm	From home to Gran's house	3 Miles	Saw a rainbow!
Sat 6/6/2016	10.00am	1.30pm	Alderley Edge Loop	15 Miles	Went with mum. Fun but really long, got tired and needed to stop!

Rainy days are still cycling days

If you're wearing the right clothing then every day is a cycling day.
But sometimes, rain and snow can make it far too cold and slippy,
so here are some fun things to do when you're snug on the sofa instead.

✿ Draw your ultimate bike

Some of the top cyclists in the world have designed their own bikes.
Remember Graeme Obree who built his record-breaking bike all by himself
with parts from a washing machine? Well, now's your chance to show off
your design skills. Think about what will work best for your kind of bike –
is it speed you need, or durability? But don't forget to have fun too. Who
wouldn't want a bike with a snack dispenser and an invisibility shield?

✿ Design your team strip

Do you have a favourite colour? Or favourite team you like to support? Why not use that as inspiration for your very own team strip. Think about what will really make you stand out from the pack. Pink and purple spots, anyone?

Write your own cycle story

Can you make up your own story about something fantastic that happens to you on your bike? Here are some top tips from Flying Fergus's awesome co-author, Joanna Nadin.

1 Think about the things a bike can be good for: chasing criminals, getting away from the school bully, or even carrying an injured puppy home quickly!

2 Every story has an 'inspirational moment' – that's what sets our hero or heroine off on their adventure. For Fergus, it's when he gets his magic bike on his birthday. What will yours be? Maybe there's a big race in town and the baddie is determined to win. Or you need a new helmet and there's a treasure hunt with a £50 prize!

3 Next, characters. Decide who your hero or heroine will be, and you'll need friends and a sidekick – maybe your own mates and your cat or dog.

4 You'll also need an 'antagonist' – better known as a baddie. They're the ones who try to stop heroes and heroines getting what they want. How will yours try to get in the way in your story?

5. Last of all you need to think about the ending. Will your story have a happy one? And what will your main character have learned on the way? Maybe they know now that telling the truth is important. Or that all the kit in the world can't buy prizes. Or that sometimes, winning isn't everything.

6. If you can't think of anything right now, why not pick three of these elements and try to come up with a story that would use them. Or you can just add one or two to your own tale:

- A CAVE
- A MAGIC GADGET
- AN EVIL MONKEY
- A DIAMOND ROBBERY
- A WHEELIE CONTEST
- A SNEAKY TEACHER
- A SLIPPERY BANANA SKIN
- A SLOW BICYCLE RACE

Cycling is always an adventure, and bikes can be brilliant when we put them in stories. That's why I came up with Flying Fergus! There's the whole series to catch up on if you haven't read them yet.

CHRIS HOY
FLYING FERGUS
The Best Birthday Bike

CHRIS HOY
FLYING FERGUS
The Great Cycle Challenge

CHRIS HOY
FLYING FERGUS
The Big Biscuit Bike Off

CHRIS HOY
FLYING FERGUS
The Championship Cheats

CHRIS HOY
FLYING FERGUS
The Winning Team

Fill in our comic strip

Are you better with pictures than words, like Fergus's fabulous illustrator Clare Elsom? Have a go at finishing her comic strip story.
What happens to Daisy and Fergus next is up to you!

WHEN	START	FINISH	WHERE I WENT	TOTAL DISTANCE	WHAT HAPPENED

WHEN	START	FINISH	WHERE I WENT	TOTAL DISTANCE	WHAT HAPPENED

LOG

WHEN	START	FINISH	WHERE I WENT	TOTAL DISTANCE	WHAT HAPPENED

LOG

WHEN	WHERE	STUNT	HOW IT WENT

FROM	TO	DISTANCE	NOTES

ANSWERS PAGE

✿ CHAPTER 1

1. Mountain bike
2. To lock shoes in place
3. Hybrid
4. Toes touching the ground
5. Recumbent bike

✿ CHAPTER 2

1. Decals
2. Wool
3. Key and combination
4.. Dynamo
5. Lights, bright clothing, bell

✿ CHAPTER 3

1. An old hot water bottle
2. Sprockets
3. Listen for air hissing or hold it under water and look for bubbles
4. Go to a repair shop – it might mean the chain is too loose, or the teeth too worn down
5. All of it

✿ CHAPTER 4

1. No motor vehicles
2. 1931
3. Extend your right arm to the side
4. Pot holes
5. If you and your bike are undamaged, then get back in the saddle as quick as you can

✿ CHAPTER 5

1. Backside or bottom
2. Up to 650
3. Protein
4. Heart
5. Calf

✿ CHAPTER 6

1. Slalom
2. Wheelie
3. Balance
4. Knock-out
5. Thinking up a great name

How did you do?

25–30 = BEAST!
10–24 = BRILLIOTIC!
0–10 = Better luck next time!

USEFUL INFORMATION

To find out more about where to go and what to do, or to get handy tips on different aspects of cycling, check out these places for more information.

BRITISH CYCLING
www.britishcycling.org.uk
A one-stop shop for everything great about cycling in Great Britain – this is where you'll find news of the GB Cycling teams, but also where you can get involved through Go-Ride clubs and sessions.

CHRIS HOY
www.chrishoy.com
Find out more about Sir Chris Hoy and his Olympic career here, and keep up to date with news and events.

CYCLING UK
www.cyclinguk.org
Great campaigns and events to get involved with in your local community from an organization that's been around for over 100 years!

FLYING FERGUS
www.flyingfergus.com
Find out more about Fergus Hamilton and the amazing adventures he gets up to on his magical bike here, and join the fan club.

NATIONAL CYCLE NETWORK
www.sustrans.org.uk
Organisers of The Big Pedal for schools, this is also the site to head to if you want to plan your cycle routes to exciting destinations or just choose the roads with the least traffic.

SKY RIDE
www.goskyride.com
Get involved with the chance to participate in traffic-free mass rides, or social guided groups in your area of the country and meet like-minded bike fans.

WHY CYCLE?
www.whycycle.co.uk
A good source of practical information and links from cycling enthusiasts.

If you want to check out the bikes and cycle gear I've designed exclusively with Evans Cycles, go to: www.evanscycles.com/Hoy

INDEX